A Neon Tryst

Lina ramona Vitkauskas

A Neon Tryst

Shearsman Books

First published in the United Kingdom in 2013 by
Shearsman Books
50 Westons Hill Drive
Emersons Green
BRISTOL
BS16 7DF

Shearsman Books Ltd Registered Office
30-31 St. James Place, Mangotsfield, Bristol BS16 9JB
(this address not for correspondence)

www.shearsman.com

ISBN 978-1-84861-236-5

Contents

Black Patent Translations
to
L'Eclisse

L'Eclisse (1962) stars the sleek-silver-hypnotic Monica Vitti as a lost woman re-discovering herself after leaving her husband. She cavorts with friends about town. She mingles with men on the stock trading floor (perhaps Antonioni's metaphor for self-worth). She has an affair with a younger man. She abandons him. It is a vague/unclear future for her in this new life. Everything is pure, fluid Vitti in this film: doe-eyed, desperate, tortured, and sophisticated.

Meditation in mirrors

She, twin nude nun,
mouths the moth wings
of the fan, lips the sun
in a slip. She repeats
to herself the chronology
of the mountain, outskirts
the windows, paperweight
stumps, cylindrical,
trumpet-bodied vases.
She is not,
she paces,
drawn to him,
but poorly formed
away from him.
The architecture of the room,
the hamlet in the portrait,
she (edible species) seeks ideals:
love's gigantic stalk.

You are an investment
Her skin framed by vellum fir
Vitti moulded hills.
She: marble-heeled in fetal position grace.
Lashes deciduously shed intent.
The moment we leave one another
is a pyramid of lemurs and tragic wind.
My life is a fungus perception.
I'm a sham, a child
I'm the socialite ignoring
black patent translations.
Her curves make rules,
like a poison cactus-brooch in the road.

In this agaric market
Trade floor manclusters
their handkerchiefs
and beds ringing with death.
These pillars from
formal families,
pressed from iron.
Money the pears,
money the love,
money the jacquard.
Finger the hermit crab,
this shelled soprano.

Lily stone man
made of books.
We stole pages
of new art,
against hammers,
against planes,
against tired threads
of women who congregate
in Nairobi as hippos, baobabs,
as *nieve*. Stay vinyl and
drum the spears.
In a trance dance,
raise your geranium
revolver. Be frothy
and rascally. Be a conifer
in dark, dense streets.

Unbearable advertisement
The gunpowder of my apartment
is a cave, a bullhorn nail in the night.
Nothing but terry robes and almond
confections. A fountain in the courtyard.
Naivasha[1] and more oily guns.
The savannah of sleep,
a thick junk blessing on the turntable,
my sleep concocts dung ruffles,
wine farms and modern clinics.

[1] A market town in Kenya.

The dogs of the neighbourhood
Love is difficult:
drunk as an upright poodle.

The unwilling foundation
Poles create angles.
Help me mend this parachute.
The doors of nimbostratus,
Coliseum against propeller,
she is found on the ground
eyeing a meadowlark, all askew
and unfamiliar.
But you. Ciao. You are new.

Dino's mini fan
Getting back to Rome
and Dino's mini fan.
It clashes with trading
screams at the ugly bell,
here he goes into the octopi pit,
into the lamp-dance of worth.
In new spectacles,
in sell-buy booths,
while she crosses herself,
a throng of cinnabar red lips
lick her frozen stare
into a permanent alone
brand.

Viscous price drop
I want to be like Pavlov,
like champagne.
In German ruins,
bonds throw a gamble
on scum, on public salmon myths,
here we are obsessed in a crowd.

Farmacia

A weightless phosphate: minerals, tokens, and movement.
Here is a man
who never stands still.

Basilica

Oh poverty!
Too sandy, too dusty,
two beads younger
than the fine, silver radio.
An industrial adding machine,
the records and stamps,
her chanterelle gills
but a payment of rotary sighs.
It's her hide to remember,
all these millions of *lire*.

A night in the business
Here come the nerves of a bat,
splayed wings and numbers
of gelato blondes. Here comes
the dark Fiat honey, the lack of
night above her brow.
He wants a replacement,
and thrusts tough language:
a rough lust latitude.

Scuba pulley
This is a simple machine:
an underwater vehicle,
a breathing apparatus.
The entire town dressed
in white, her bolete body
kissed by a passing drunk.
The town's cranes, sprinklers,
palms, squares, and refusals.
His instigation produces tawny milk caps.

Balloon

At the crosswalk-catwalk-caterwaul she slows, she calculates,
he says he will kiss her in the brush, in the rain barrel, maul her
back to her mother, he goes, she goes, naked sunflowers and a
torn strap, the listless light. *Paese Sera*[2] across her roused body,
she broods across the news, *the model buildings, oh all the white
model buildings...*

[2] A Communist Italian newspaper.

Wicker clouds

Carmel Coral is too vulnerable
for a ring, for a new car, for a husband!
Not in my bed,
not down my drain.
I look for absolutes:
this walnut door is absolute,
the placid cleaning woman
is absolute, a man boxing
passionately with a model
ship is absolute.
Here I am immaculate
as Nana's tablecloths, all are absolute.
We sex for the keyhole game.

We wake with a church far off
In an affair,
arms laugh,
they become sheer.

Doorbell

Thin wristwatch through the medical door
a peppery choice! This peacock toxic love.
Here in the office of one thousand telephones.

Maid mushroom
The ejaculatory tinker
reveals the rain barrel twice
a couple teen horses
barking out and baring
menacing faces of bus passengers
LA GARA ATOMICA
a telescopic clover
but all this doesn't mean love.

Maid mushroom
Couples into streets trickle into gutters here they wash
winter away between stones, pre-Brakhage.

Wilson, 722
to
Seconds

Seconds (1966) stars Rock Hudson as an aging, bored, East-coast man who is encouraged to commit pseudocide by an ominous group of wealthy men called "The Company." After being framed by "The Company" (he is doped and filmed raping a girl) he literally becomes—via reconstructive surgery—a new person. His new identity, a hip, young emerging artist who resides in a beach house on the California coast, offers him fabulous opportunities: women, parties, and acceptance. All of the adulation, however, catches up to him and he is found out. As punishment, he must go back to his old life.

Face

The face is a perilous thing,
an exercise in longevity,
a sterile whey pool,
the lips a salty mirror,
eyes skewed as butter pats,
an opening in the mask,
a sock-cotton map,
a raving monster in the plaza,
an orchid in a hat waiting
at the turnstile, an expert in
the crowd following the face.
Steps upon ceramic, molten
earlobes and machinery; a ticket
stub, a wet condom.
The train pulls away
into the tunnel,
an unread newspaper:
Arthur Hamilton.

Track 25
We cannot see this on the billboard,
but the conductor has a dollar
in his scandalous mouth.
Arthur Hamilton peeks from the window,
a partridge under the fluorescent,
his story in his suit coat pocket,
a guidebook.

34 Lafayette Street

Violins crinkle behind Arthur Hamilton,
in the meadow behind him,
in the glassy crossword,
in the stance of all men.
You see, here is the beginning:
a prison of clocks, crescents of heads.

Sweat pours down his cheeks
Scarsdale. We've arrived.
I stayed up all night defending myself.
A polite kiss to my wife.
I unearthed her tropic roses,
produced for her the feel of things,
created my daughter, the siren.
Smoke rings from my study,
the cradle's smirk off the hook,
now my dear, dead friend
calling me, culling me
from radioactive reticence.

The trophies near the fireplace

Our wristwatches match.
The doubles match at Princeton.
Do you remember, Arthur?
Fidelis Eternis[3]
You are Wilson
and I'm Charlie.
I'm alive.
Please come, Arthur.
You caught this,
in the finned negligée,
in your net; you've wrangled all
the items in your tackle box
and pinned them like a Navajo
to the ache of a skiff's damp curves.
Do you remember, Arthur,
this limp receiver trout?

[3] Latin: "Faithful Always."

Cross-examination
I understand perfectly as your wife and
I know, you are sorry.
Your stony scaled kiss
below the mantle.
We lie awake
like crusting crabs
under cold suns.

Your present equity
The grey of reappraisal.
The deliberate steaming cranium.
The elders press shirts in a caged room,
muscles, seams, and catapults.
Do you know me?
My tie is immaculate.
Fans whir, the knives of summer.
This is where to go—into the meat.

Hook off
Coming in, move that beef!
Already in your iron curiosity.
Customers ride in back.
"Honest Arnie", Used Cow Dealer.
To your left, sir.
Wood grain, long hallways, white jackets.
Yellow ladders, machines in the park.
To your left, sir.

Initiation
Jacquard walls
and you in black.
Your skin
against checkerboards.
The scene requires
me to pull pieces
from you as if we
were in a bazaar
of punctual snakes.
I have to half you.

I am like a jaguar in this classroom
No one will speak to me.
No one will speak to me.
No one will speak to me.

I love this nude from a distance
The question of death selection
may be the most important in your life.
Impaled by rain, the memory
of dinner, of flesh, of stitches;
all have a rubber hunger.
Indelicate questions
and a Roquefort complexion,
the circumstances of your death
must be simple. The trick lies
in obliterating just so much
and no more.
You collect collarbone
vignettes, cigarettes, pirouettes;
your city an entire impervious
velvet instrument of certified
endings and logarithms.
We guarantee a death
of this kind: an explosion,
a hunting misadventure,
a hotel room fire.
I cannot change who I am,
only who I am when
I have changed myself.
Note: this chicken is delicious.

My face / tile floor
Trust the silver instruments.
Your new identity.
Accept and sign for it.
I see the curdled plastic
projection. Here I am
with her, the bluebell girl,
the wife misshapen as a
Neptunian statue
into disastrous disability,
the minted daughter,
a trump or
someone else.
I did not ravage
their girl, I open my statement
wide. But, fair enough,
I rebirth.

What have I done?
I can never go back.
Never a lye bowtie again.
Out West my daughter
is riding her husband,
a doctor she wrung
and blazed upon him
a brand and saddled him;
she loves to crease him,
feel the strength of his
calloused, surgical hands
upon her plow-girl spine.
I remember, as I pushed her
on the tire and back,
folded my arms in the wind
like thin cigars wincing
in the curdled Scarsdale night,
damp with stiff, bleach orgasms.

I expect to be president of the bank
Anything at all?
Anything at all?
I realize Emily masturbates in the bath.
I realize we hardly ever quarrel.
We are hard-graphed.
Hardly ever.
We have a boat.

Sign here
A struggle in the soul of a good man
that wasn't hard
A struggle in the soul of a good man
shows no diagrams,
smells of youth becoming rock,
chiseled and planned,
injected, conglomerate.
The tin-clamor cleansing
of instruments.
I cannot breathe
my mouth sewn and milestone teeth
ground as an obituary.
When I soon prance around
like a stud bull
but my vocal chords, that's what hurts most right now.

The mandible

Well, I never.

Hematoma

Get me to where I need to be.
Condition my muscle and signature.
I want a ball. A big, big, red one.
Abroad, *my pictures are realistic*
in treatment but deal with poetic imagery
in choice of subject.
False artisan,
call me a cutlet of my throat,
grunt me a wish to be old again.
Do I know a brush as well as my own loneliness?
I am forged. Already established.
Mildly successful.
Surreal, primitive, impressionist, whatever.
I am accepted.

My own new dimension
Alone in the world,
(Giddy laughter)
Isn't it marvelous?
Malibu privates. Privates. Precious beach breasts.
Private privates. Private-alone-privates.
Every middle-aged man in America
wants a pillowed plane,
to be handsome in profile.

New woman
Scarsdale again.
Alfred in briefcase solitude.
Comfortable.
Well, I like my studio.
Hot air balloon trivets,
a woman splayed open
on my kitchen floor,
sex with paint.
The bath is through here.
Emily. Her wilting, dried tulip,
though clearly submerged.
The shine of my teeth upon sand.

You may have problems at first
Globe patio pool,
Marilyn drowned after *The Misfits*.
Cocktails embellish my posture,
surround my easel and signature.
Rags, turpentine, professionals.
So I attempt form and figure.
Tea suggestions urge socialization.
Walk-by blonde beach, waves
and the gardener of bougainvillea.
Does it grow here?
My shaved angles. My mirrors
like Nabokov's *Guide to Berlin*.
Glass man coming through,
waving reflective man with brush!
I paint with conviction, but I am not ready.
Now these pallid dunes and tobacco.
She.

Nora Marcus
Do I know this walk? This rock?
Her bare feet in ocean,
all the power.
Mind her
and chop her
with two boys,
complete with
microwave oven.
Kitchen floor
face
rain.
Finishing
the hurt.
She is so sweater,
she is so weather,
she knows I null myself
impure, that I am tentative.
Unturned.
Her teeth just like everyone's.
It is very nice here.
The good things always happen with the rain.

Convertible Dionysius

What do you do with a drunken sailor?
Where's the wild-wine-nipple Renaissance?
Here.
She fucks everyone's accordions, flutes, and laurels.
Rock Hudson, I break you into coronets.
She in grapeseed residue pressed against fertile bodies,
braless bosoms, rosy-buttocked as Anne Boleyn.
She slips off her white dress
and rubs me in Santa Barbara:
a new model of a barrel life, laughing.
I don't know any of these people.
I'm dying and that's the world.

It's not like you
Martini, I promise,
Carpet, curtain, embarrassment.
I work for them. Now it is time
to kiss you, keep you tempered
reveal you while reveling in you.
God, how evil I am.
Let's laugh until panties.
Until theft.
Henry Bushbain went to Harvard!
He's a sneaky two-face, that Henry.
Here we introduce virgin sacrifices.
I just love your paintings, Mr. Wilson, just how do you do it?
Well, you see, it all started with a big red ball.

I paint naked, Mrs. Filter
God, that will never come out.
It will never come out.
I am sure it will never/all come out.

All of your faces like a tackle team
I was an alumnus, yes!
We are dashing into blue obscurity...
Does Wilson play golf?
You don't have a nephew.
Plaid sheets.
Does Wilson play golf?
My daughter is married to a doctor.
Does Wilson play golf?
Why are you all staring at me like that?
Our host is in orbit.

Now I know blonde means nothing,
means Dead Man's Curve,
means Beach Blanket Bingo.
We're sort of tied together,
you and me.
Emily.
In our Colonial home,
pristine.
Those years
like a music box ballerina
in the garage
silenced by watercolor pearls.
I am so glad you were able to come.
I hope I've been of some help.

Memento

Trophy unwrapped.
Brown wrapper legs.
Alfred opened me on my old street.
It just doesn't matter.
The company does not see me.

Begin again
Mistakes were made in my case.
It's a word-of-mouth operation.
Balloon documentation.
A 13-1/2 inch bicep.
A classroom where the trophies
and buddies opt in.
You don't need to be intimately acquainted with a man
to realize he'd be receptive to the type of opportunity we offer.

Into the Black Flocks
to
Wild Strawberries

Bergman's classic film, *Wild Strawberries* (1957), tells the tale of an aged, retired professor travelling cross-country to his alma mater to receive a lifetime achievement award. Accompanying him on his travels is his soon-to-be daughter-in-law who resents him. Along the way they pick up a fighting couple and young students of religion and philosophy.

Character and behavior

Age is a cigarette,
an arrow to science.
The library daises
become a uniform,
a new Swedish shame.
I am grateful for my love
of chemistry. If men in Lund,
if we are miles away in a bleached
memory, no bare children
bask gilded in daylight.
Aurora strains through
the damask, a burn on the
forehead of truth, my wife
(not my housekeeper)
winces flame and circus snout.
My name is Isak Borg and I am 78.
I'll be at the cathedral tomorrow.

Smultronstället[4]

The dream of an empty street.
So many of us in iron furs,
myself in vicious life, no one
of wood or autumn or ribs
can undo the stiff cloaked clock.
It reminds.
Here a horse trades me
into lint, grommets, a casket.
Cobblestone faceless me,
disintegrating sockets against
the fence. Slowly a fish labels
the moment, the wheel unravels,
pouring itself down the street.

[4] Swedish: "Wild strawberries"

Moustache alarm
A broken carriage
of hands grasping fists of wet
leaving, the stoic port painting,
the sunlight assumes me; I must dress,
amble to the crispy housekeeper,
cradle candles in order to sleep.
I am the same, please myself.
Yourself. I could be at the airport
in Malmo, a glass of water,
Agda, we are not married.
Is that your last word?

Packing

Eggs, you honorary idiot!
Calm the old girl.
Flies on toast,
a blossoming lily lamp.
If house plants and curtains,
if hail storms by my daughter-in-law,
who is nor city nor pine woman,
if flies on toast.
And men have vices,
men have vices.

I can't stand chalets
We need to pay you back,
we can never be free,
Evald respects that,
and he hates you.
The road lines are frank
and you
are ruthless.
Loops and whorls
of old manners and charm.
The cushioned rear window
yawns Nordic.
I have no respect for mental suffering.
Inside my mouth,
I am not interested in dreams.
Through the countryside,
we pick up the young
travelers in the forest first.
She goes strawberry picking
and you
reminisce,
get sentimental
in the foliage
where you played as a child,
free to dissolve love.
Your clouded, ivy pupils
burn. We sit at the table,
our uncle stone deaf
with midnight horn pressed
to his ear, horn of unwanted kisses.
Of regret.

The cousins' love
You are beautiful.
He is the nicest.
The twins know most things
when you blush.
A kiss in the bluebells,
stained with "bad" woman.
My apron flush
with the barn in the distance.
Pond laundress,
a mother meadow girl
don't wait in your own mirage.
Unscroll yourself upon the drunk
wall stripes,
flailing braids and bows
hats and tails.

Fingernails filthy in the butter
of love,
the gong
of food, the deaf
tube
again.
Love is drying
uncle's name day,
a creamed
soup of wrens.
I have the picture, Anna ashamed, crying.
He talks about poetry and the next life!
He is a child and I am bold.

Cockleshell man
with grassy ornamental brows,
where was I?
Awakened from my reveries,
travelers approaching.
Italian traveler flanked
by religion and science
and luggage tie
strangling me in the sun,
her shady virgin cheeks;
my pipe.
You were like Sara in her youth.

The accident

I have been hurting my knees my whole life.
Women must remain flipped in ditches.
It was my wife who caused this accident,
intrusive curves appeared. The car lifted
an ache of all travelers, the rope strain
of husbands, you will have hot showers,
a stroke, a mane, a woman named
Marianne takes the wheel.
A blanket of beetles surviving smashes,
stares. *She made me believe she had cancer,*
the doctors found nothing wrong with her.

Afford the heat

She cracks his stopwatch
as he explodes indifferently.
Among children
they fight, she a cricket
in the road, he, tomorrow's needle.
Tomorrow the movie continues,
the adventure continues,
going to Marfak
and mother
continues.
The gas station attendant
knows the doctor, they still discuss
one another, name their children
under sticky hoods, licking what rain is left.
I'll be the godfather.

Look for Caltex, view the vista blank,
lunch with the officers,
out of gooseberry goblets.
Give me the courtesy,
recite poetry
talk of no gods
or science.
Your rationalism
is dust, modern man
is a figment in the wildflowers.
Where is the friend
I seek at the break of day?
When night falls,
I still have not found Him
I see traces wherever
flowers bloom, his love
mingles with every air.

An aviary in Stockholm
Some of your toys,
says mother,
were always silk stranglers.
I have Sigbritt's doll,
I made the dress myself.

Blind eyes in the train ashtray,
antique talk
the perfect flypaper
belles against a handless
watch, again your tie
in the sand clams,
in the lilac arbor,
the whiteness
of your mother's hair,
unable to shawl
lips to collar,
chimneys and flags,
they started arguing about God.

Dozing off

Unlanguage our blessings.
Listen as a professor.
You know so much and know nothing.
Her striped dress
as she runs through sheets,
rotten baby in a curdled bassinet,
her curls succeeding
your twisted branch.
Here the life breathes into the black flocks.

These holes at room temperature,
sheer curtains against the nape
of her piano, upon linen neck,
a Blanche Dubois forcing darkness
upon her suitors, controlling them
in a farce of barn nails,
clean windows,
rays of sun stigmata.
In Borg, a handkerchief
plus a locket,
born of celery stalks
and where are the children?

At the chalkboard
Identify the microorganism.
Behind wood slats, crates,
examine this specimen.
Identify the microorganism.
Wrong intake.
A glass eyed linguist.
Identify the microorganism.
Know your doctor's duty.
Ask forgiveness.
Reach for a telegraph.
Guilt the dead.
Identify the microorganism.
Water interrogative.
A verdict clean medical table.
A selfish cadaver.
Identify the microorganism.

The swamp moss, the rusted ladder
Laugh into the taffeta wood.
Steal lip shade in the tines
of unraveled hair, push yourself
into the clearing.
Resistance is a board,
laugh a pop of ice
among tenderized digits,
each number a calculated
sweet, an emerald lisp of jealousy.

Freize

Surgical precision is love
removed from the usual hooks.
I am the river,
and Marianne smokes.
A tartan window,
and here, picking wildflowers
from the professor's steering
wheel, the galaxies continue
to promise.
The sea is setting is sitting she said
she was pregnant she said, raised her petals
in the hospital, the coward's life of raincoats.
The faculty flung onto the walls
in flesh Braille, taut stairs of man,
of woman, to live and create life and man
to be dead, stone-dead.

Birch lurch
Gasp goat in steeples,
mother of light years,
growing near the ivy bed,
the misery marriage bouquet.
A doctor, everything in the heart
getting late, the heads of pastries
all aligned.

University fences

You spoiled the suitcase,
and here is Evald,
a guest room man symmetrical and ripping.
He is pleasant.
Our cabinets immaculate.
Your new shoelaces
a banquet trumpet.
The ceremony medals,
the procession, the stale
daylight upon spectacles
and buckles. The sashes
in the cathedral, butterbean
bows, sardines, and queens.
In straying white,
a jumble of saints,
their heads sewn
with diplomas,
my housemaid's woolen robe.

Draw, paste, show me

Our electric puts a marker on us.
We should know how to behave.
The lagoon's serenade,
you know me,
wistful.
The last gardener triumph,
our apricots tender, splendid, and proud.
On we go Hamburg,
to have a grassy-lush-lazy.
I hear your backbone,
it turns smoke
so strident at my bedside.

Pillow house
Nor papa
nor mama
nor anyone,
all overboard.
The doll fish,
a porkpie hat,
a last embroidered memory
upon buttons,
the door cracked
in catatonic sweat.

CPSIA information can be obtained at www.ICGtesting.com
Printed in the USA
LVOW131127201212

312525LV00001B/3/P